EBOOK ASSETS

WRITING A BOOK

Shortcuts Made Easy

Writing A Book – Shortcuts Made Easy

Published by Ebook Assets

Copyright © 2016 by Ebook Assets

Visit us on the Web

www.ebookassets.com

Table of Contents

"To gain your own voice, you have to forget about having it heard."

- Allen Ginsberg, WD

Chapter 1

When it comes to writing a strong ebook, this can be a very intimidating thing for new authors. The problem is that some writers go into writing books as if there are strict rules that need to be followed. When it comes to learning how to write, you need to understand the most important rule of all: there are no rules. If you pressure yourself by following the processes learned in creative writing classes, you are going to get writer's block and you will become overly frustrated with the topic. For instance, writing linearly may be what you were taught to do but that may not necessarily work for you.

One of the best writing tips for your first eBook is to just write. You do not have to start from the beginning of the book and end at the ending. You can start halfway through if you know what events are going to lead up to the ending of your book. If you know how the book is going to end, you can start with that and move backwards. You can even piece together chapters and write as you come up with ideas and string them together later. Sometimes you are able to accomplish writing from beginning to end. You need to allow yourself the freedom to just write without hindering yourself. This is the best way for making writing easy for new authors. The minute you free yourself of these perceived rules, the minute you can write on stress-free.

Everyone has different ideas on writing. Writing is an art and no art form should really have rules to follow. Rules hurt creativity and writers need to have the creative freedom to do what they need to in order to complete their book. Even any new approaches to writing can be suffocating for writers. Your brain flows ideas at its own pace and you need to let your creative mind do what it needs to. Eventually, everything will come together exactly how you intend it to, so write as you need to. You can go back and improve the flow of your story after you get the main points of your manuscript done and out of the way first. Who cares that you started writing your book at chapter 4 and went to chapter 6, then went back to chapter one. Spoiler alert: the readers only care about the end product.

Chapter 1

You need to be free when you are writing your book. The minute that you start pressuring yourself with rules to writing your book or strict deadlines, you are going to get writer's block and you will ultimately be unhappy with your final product. This is something that could turn you off from the writing process all together. When you take a more carefree approach to writing, you will find that things will flow a lot more easily from your brain to your fingertips. As long as you make sure the story flows together, you can really write in any order that you get your ideas for.

Chapter 2

Writer's block is the absolute worst thing that could possibly happen, not just when you are writing your first book but any book that follows it. Actually, having your computer go down is the worst, but writer's block is definitely a very close second. Becoming a writer and how to write amazing books is really only half the battle. You also must overcome this dreaded writer's block, the bane of any writer's existence. One of the best eBook writing tips that you can get to help you get around writer's block is to have more than one project to focus on.

This may seem like madness to you. However, this does not mean that you do not completely have your focus on your primary project. One of the new approaches of writing is to work on two or more projects at any given time, which may seem counterproductive but you may be surprised at the benefits of this. To explain why this works, let's go back to your time at school. Whenever you were studying or doing homework, what would you do? Quite likely, you moved onto another topic or assignment when you got stuck and you did this for 2 reasons. One reason is that you didn't want to waste all of your time on one paper that would slow you down, making it so that you couldn't get through all of your assignments in time. Another reason is that by going back to it, you can have a fresh mind which will help you think better.

When you are writing a book, you will inevitably get stuck. You could sit there and frustrate yourself further by obsessing over this, which will only worsen your writer's block and may even make you want to quit the book all together. Instead of getting yourself all worked up over this, you can just move onto one of your other projects. This project doesn't need to be another big novel. It could be a short story, an article, or even some poetry. By switching around from project to project when you get stuck, you can ease your frustration about your lack of productivity but you can also get back to your original novel with fresh eyes that will help you to get over your block. It really sounds crazy but this is easily one of the best tips on writing you can get when it comes to overcoming the dreaded writer's block.

This is something that has actually been proven thanks to cognitive psychology. When researching the best way to go about studying and schoolwork, they discovered that this very same principle will help someone become a better student. This is because it relieves anxiety and frustration while also giving the student fresh eyes to go over their work with. This gives them a better chance at success. This is also going to give you the fresh perspective that you need in order to finish your book. Focus and dedication are crucial to getting things down, but sometimes you need to move onto something else for a little bit to get that focus back.

Chapter 3

You fully understand the importance of having a book that is edited before putting it out on the market to sell. Another one of the great writing tips for your first eBook and any other that follows is to make sure that your book is edited. Sure, you can pay a professional editor but this can be expensive. This means that you cannot count one someone else to be your own editor. You need to step up and take the time to look over your work. It is not the responsibility of anyone else, especially when you do not have the resources to pay for those services.

Writing a strong first novella can be very dependent on this. Your first book will establish your place in the market. Knowing how to write is completely different from knowing how to edit your own work. Remember how before it was discussed about coming up with new projects to help you have options to switch to in order to stave off the writer's block that you will inevitably face. It can be an ideal option to save your editing for just these moments.

The problem with editing right after you finish wrote the book is that it is so fresh in your mind, you know exactly what it is supposed to say in your mind and you may overlook mistakes. Then, you will think that your book is perfect and release it. However, that is usually not the case. In fact, editing your book a few different times can make sure that it is absolutely perfect. You need to keep editing to get your eBook exactly right.

You should return to your book a few times in between projects. Every time you come back to it after working on something else, you will return with fresh eyes to edit your book. You may be surprised how many mistakes you will find even after the second time returning to your book. You will definitely be surprised that there are even mistakes after your third time looking at your book. It is a long process to thoroughly edit a book. It is a perfect way to both complete your editing and to overcome your writer's block at the very same time. Multi-tasking is exactly what you need to do in order to get everything done.

Having an eBook that is edited well before it is released can make a huge difference in the eventual success of your book. There are different ideas on writing but everyone agrees that books must be as perfect as possible. People want a polished final product and that does not magically happen. You must assume that it is your sole job to fix any errors in your work. Editing services can be expensive but if that is something that you are able to invest in, it can be a great idea for you. However, most new and young writers do not have that luxury and need to put in this hard work themselves.

Chapter 4

When your eBook is released out into the world, you face the harsh criticisms head on. This can be blindsiding for people who have not had anyone critique their book before their eBook. That first set of bad reviews can frustrate you and maybe turn you off entirely from the process. One of the best writing tips that you can get is to get someone or some people to read your book before you release it. This is something that will really make a huge difference in the quality of your work.

Writers should send out their works for people to read before releasing their book. The problem is in the "who" in this scenario. People often make a huge mistake of sending out their book to their friends and family. These are people that are emotionally invested in you and they do not want to hurt your feelings. It is like when you wear an outfit that may not look great on you or you try a new hairstyle. They will sugar-coat how they feel about it as to not hurt your feelings. That will not help you in any way. This will certainly not prepare you in case you get really harsh comments about your eBook.

After you finish writing your first eBook, you should find someone that you know will be completely honest with you about your book. This could be a friend that you know will always be brutally honest or through a professional writer or editor. Give them the go-ahead to say exactly what they are thinking about your book. Let them be harsh with you because as much as it may sting a little, it will be good for you. This is how you get better and how you grow as an artist. Constructive criticism is a necessity to make sure that your product is perfect before you start sending it out. When you go out into the real world of writing, you will face a great deal of rejection and you will face criticism. It can be a very disheartening world out there and you can be much better prepared for it if you are critiqued before then. This is important to becoming a writer and how to write more effectively. You may find that people have different ideas on writing but you can get a good idea of how your book will perform and any changes that you need to make.

Now one wants to feel awful about any art that they put out there. Writing is really just another art form that is criticized or praised on a wide level. Getting too much criticism, especially for a new author, can be a bad thing for your budding writing career. However, getting this criticism on your own terms can be quite beneficial to increasing your writing skill. There are people that are born with a natural talent for writing, but if you do not work towards growing in your craft you will run the risk of never excelling.

Chapter 5

Social media is a big thing right now. In fact, as one of the new approaches to writing, writers use social media as a way to connect with their fans and raise awareness for their works. Social media has really changed the landscape, especially for writers who are publishing eBooks on their own. If you look at your phone right now, you probably have Pinterest, Facebook, Twitter, and Instagram apps on your phone that you actually use on a regular basis. All of your friends have all of these social media accounts. In fact, your parents even use them. However, social media is as much of a curse as it is a blessing for any writer.

First, let's look at the positives of using social media. Most importantly, social media is an incredible (and for the most part free) way to promote your brand and your work. You may be asking "I'm a writer; what is my brand?" The brand is you. You want to connect with users by showing off your wit when writing social media posts. You want to draw attention to your hard work or your author page on whichever eBook platform you choose to go with. Having an online presence is essential to being a successful self-published author. You will gain a positive reputation that will help you get noticed more on search engines. Social media has the potential to be your best friend.

Social media could also be your worst enemy. Imagine that you are writing your first book. You may have a lull that leads you to your phone to look through your social media accounts or lead you online to head to them. Then you find yourself reading for hours, going from news story or to look something up that you saw on someone's Facebook. That is enough of a waste of time, which does not even take into consideration the time you will likely end up spending playing Candy Crush. The next thing you know, you completed 2 sentences of chapter 1 but wasted hours of great working time on social media. There is a reason why workplaces block these sites. Social media is a proven productivity killer and you do not want to be the one to suffer from this. Social media can definitely get in the way of writing a strong first novella or really anything else that you may want to do.

As a writer, you need to be as productive as possible. Limit your time on social media and even block access to these things yourself. Treat your writing as you would your job. Plan a time that you are going to dedicate to your work and stick to that time. For instance, if you choose to write between 12 and 5, dedicate your time between those hours on nothing else but working on your writing. If you stray from this and find yourself on social media, you could distract yourself and never get anything done. Unplugging yourself and focusing on your writing is one of the great tips for writing today.

Chapter 6

When people accomplish any type of art, there is always that "art is subjective" discussion that is tossed around. In reality, art is definitely subjective but there are some things that are just obviously bad to the rest of the world. It is not a matter of whether or not someone "got it" or was "too dumb to understand what is going on" but rather there is a questionable quality to the piece that is actually undeniable for most people to see. This applies to every piece of art, whether it is in the realm of visual or in the art of writing.

There are some writers that really just have the gift of writing. They are not perfectly honed, but with enough experience and education they can definitely get there. Then there is the bad writing. This is the writing that people do not know is bad when they are learning how to write and are never corrected. Becoming a writer and how to write are talents that people are born with but they need to be practiced as any other gift needs to be. If you don't practice your craft, you are never going to become exceptional. And let's be honest here: not everyone is very good at it.

Everyone has different ideas on writing. Some people prefer some of the new approaches to it while others prefer a more classical approach. This is completely normal. However, the quality is really where the problem exists. Maybe a person did not have professional editing done or have someone be honest about the quality of their book. Whatever the reason is, this person ends up releasing their book and it is less than stellar. More often than not, this comes as a huge shock to them. That is when they become defensive and start using the "art is subjective" line.

One of the big tips on writing is to make sure that you are putting out a quality product. You do not want to put out something for the sake of putting something out. Duke Wellington once said that "There are two kinds of music: good music, and the other kind." This same principle applies to books and you do not want to be put in the category of "the other kind", especially when you are writing your first book and publishing it. First impressions are big in any industry and this first novel could be a pivotal moment that will make or break your budding career.

There are bad books and there are great ones. Not every book that you release is going to be the next "Wuthering Heights" but you could certainly avoid being the book that no one ever wants to read. You are trying to build up your brand and as a writer this means making sure that you are putting out books that are high quality with fantastic writing that draws the reader in. You want to be memorable, not forgettable.

Chapter 7

When you go into a coffee shop, you probably notice a large amount of the people in these shops have their tablets or laptops out and they are working on something. Some of those people are working on projects and homework for school, but there are a large amount of people that are writers trying to write the next great American novel. This is the hip thing write now, but is it the right thing for you to do when you are writing your first book? Maybe you should reconsider your café workplace and get something a bit more intimate.

There is a reason why people who work at an office tend to have their own private workspace. This is a productive way to get your tasks done and this is why people need their own private space. When you are in a public place like a coffee shop, you are exposing yourself to distractions in the outside world that may actually be a hindrance to the writing process. People may constantly come up to you and ask you what they are working on. Others may just be too loud that it distracts you. This is why it is incredibly important for you to treat your book as a job and give yourself the workspace that you need and deserve to get your book done.

This is the perfect way for making writing easy for new authors. A more experienced author may be able to block out these distractions better than someone who is just really happy to be getting out there for the first time writing their book. When you have your own private space, you can make as much or as little of a mess that you want. You can close the door for complete silence from the outside world. You can play whatever music really gets the creative juices rolling when you are trying to work. You have a lot more freedom when working at a desk at home in your own little space. You can wear sweatpants and move around the room to sit in any position that you want to help with the creativity. This does not mean a place like a coffee shop or bar doesn't have a place for the writing process. Maybe you need a chance of scenery to get rid of a nagging case of writer's block. Maybe you want to get out there to observe something to help you untie a knot that you seem to be stuck in. These places have their own spot in the writing world, but you will most benefit from a private space to call your own to work in.

Writers already inherently have difficulty with their craft. They wind around stories and get writer's block so bad that they end up focusing on every distraction rather than redirecting their attention back to the task at hand. For this reason, a person can greatly benefit from having their own little haven to write to their heart's content.

Chapter 8

If you are going to be a serious writer, you cannot just do it once in a while. Being a serious writer is not like when you say that you are going to train for a marathon but only get 2 weeks in the 10 week training program. It takes some serious dedication, otherwise you are just some part-time writer that may or may not ever release a book. If that is fine with you, then this writing tip may not be for you. If you do want to be serious, rest on for one of the best eBook writing tips.

This doesn't mean that you should quit your day job and go broke while you focus on your writing. That is, unless of course that you can afford to make this career change. But, it does take a lot of time every day to dedicate to honing your craft in order to be the best writer that you possibly can. You do not always have to write for the same book every day. You can do some poems one day or some short stories another day. What is the most important is that you spend every day writing something. You will only get out of it what you put into it, and you want to make sure that you are pouring a lot of yourself into it.

Practice makes perfect. This is one of those tips on writing that you do not want to forget. When you write for a substantial portion of every day, you are honing your craft and turning it into something that is incredible and perfect. You can only do this if you are practicing every day. You may wonder about how much time this will take. Realistically, this will take a huge chunk of your time. It is still possible to have a life and another job and write seriously. This will take some careful planning on your side. You need to make yourself a schedule and stick to it as you would your own work schedule. When you treat your writing as if it were your job, you are going to find that you are far more dedicated to it than you would be if you adopted a "well, let's try to get a little something done today" once in a while attitude. This will make a huge difference in your quality of skill when you start writing your first eBook.

You will need to dedicate a lot of time to your writing. This is the only way that you are going to get better at it. A star baseball player may be able to get up and do well but to really become a legend; they need to work to hone their specific craft. Becoming a writer and how to write well is something that you really need to work towards. Otherwise, you will never get better. There are a lot of writers out there but the ones that put the time in will stand out to readers.

Chapter 9

Whenever you tell someone that you are a writer or that your job is writing, you often get a few different reactions. Some will snort, saying that it isn't a real job. Others will act interested but are secretly judging you and making starving artist jokes in their head. Some will pretend to accept that this is your actual job, but never actually get it. There are people that will be very supportive and understanding, but you may find that for the most part people are not so accepting. The fact is that this is your job and you need to treat it as such.

When you schedule a certain amount of time per day to write, you need to stick to that schedule. This doesn't mean that you have to go straight from 9 to 5 every day, as long as you put the time in. This time is absolutely sacred just as it is as if you were clocking into work to get your paycheck. One of the big tips on writing is to stick to this allotted time if you intend on being a serious writer. You need to plan out deadlines and hours to be worked each day and you need to stand your ground and stick to them. Putting the hours is non-negotiable, despite what other people try to tell you. If they do not take your craft seriously, that does not mean you can neglect your responsibilities and stand your ground against this people that are not taking you seriously. This is important to you and you need to make sure that everyone knows it. Otherwise, what is the point in writing a strong first novella if you are going to treat it as if you were just painting for a hobby? This is not a hobby.

There really are different ideas on writing and these ideas are what make people act the way they do to you when they hear that you are writing your first eBook. Do not let people treat you like you are less than you are because they do not take you seriously and do not let them talk you into ignoring your writing for things that they need. This obviously doesn't mean that you have to ignore a big game for your child or important appointments, but these are things that you can work your schedule around rather than just not doing any writing during the day. You do have some flexibility but you do need to remember to put in the hours. If you say that you are going to work 4-6 hours on your writing, make sure that over the course of the day that you stick to this time. You can go over but this needs to be the bare minimum of what you are working with. If people have a problem with this, you do not need that kind of negativity in your life. They need to accept that your writing time is as serious as their time at work.

Chapter 10

There are so many different tips about writing. Some of the best tips on writing have already been discussed. However, it is very hard to pinpoint exactly what the best eBook writing tips actually are. There are definitely things that will make some writers stand apart from others in the industry and you can be one of those that stand apart. With this one tip, you can overcome writer's block and finishing writing your first eBook. The answer to becoming a writer and how to write incredible things comes with following the three "P's".

The first question that you may have is what exactly these three "P's" are. They are patience, perseverance, and purpose. At the end of the day, how successful you are writing your first book will really depend on how well you follow these principles. Writing takes patience. You will not write a masterpiece in a week. That is not how things really work. Even if you do manage to complete the writing your piece in a short time, you still have to go through the editing process. Editing the book could take a fair amount of time, maybe even more time than it took you to write the piece originally. You also need patience to overcome writer's block, which seems like an obstacle too grand to overpass but you can do it with patience. You need perseverance. You need to persevere over those obstacles like writer's block or the people that think what you are doing is a joke. You need to persevere that your book will eventually get done even when fate seems to have gotten in the way with your goal.

Finally, you need to have purpose. Purpose is going to be the thing that helps you fight against things that test your patience and is what will help you persevere. When you maintain your sense of purpose, you can find that nothing will stand in your way. You will have the integrity that will come through in your work and you can be satisfied that you accomplished exactly what you have set out to do. Patience and perseverance are actions that help you to complete your goal of writing a strong first novella but purpose is the car that you took that drove you there. Purpose is what is behind this entire process. Purpose is what made you write your book. And maintaining that purpose is what will make you follow through with everything. You need your sense of purpose if you are going to keep moving forward with your writing.

There are so many different ideas on writing that each person will do things their own way. You need to remember these 3 principles if you are going to be a successful writer. If you can remember these 3 things, you will find that you can overcome anything to get your writing done. A lot of writers struggle with writing but you can do it when you follow these writing tips.

Ebook Assets

Our goal at Ebook Assets is to help new authors hone their craft and build a business. Not only do we want you to become a better writer, we want you to become a smarter business owner. Remember, authorship is a business, your assets can be both digital and paper. Together, we can help you achieve your writing goals by keeping you up to date with the latest trends and technologies.

Visit Us On The Web.

www.ebookassets.com